20TH CENTURY *music*
1960s
THE AGE OF ROCK

Please visit our web site at: www.garethstevens.com
For a free color catalog describing Gareth Stevens Publishing's list of high-quality books
and multimedia programs, call 1-800-542-2595 or fax your request to (414) 332-3567.

Library of Congress Cataloging-in-Publication Data

Hayes, Malcolm.
    1960s: the age of rock / by Malcolm Hayes.
      p. cm. — (20th century music)
    Includes bibliographical references and index.
    Summary: Discusses the influence of people and events worldwide in the 1960s which
  led to electronic experimentation, the blues, hard bop, protest songs, soul, and radical
  modernism in classical music.
    ISBN 0-8368-3034-2 (lib. bdg.)
    1. Music—20th century—History and criticism—Juvenile literature. [1. Music—20th
  century—History and criticism.] I. Title. II. 20th century music.
  ML3928.H345   2002
  780'.9'04—dc21   2001054226

This North American edition first published in 2002 by
Gareth Stevens Publishing
A World Almanac Education Group Company
330 West Olive Street, Suite 100
Milwaukee, WI 53212 USA

Original edition © 2001 by David West Children's Books. First published in Great Britain
in 2001 by Heinemann Library, Halley Court, Jordan Hill, Oxford OX2 8EJ, a division of Reed
Educational and Professional Publishing Limited. This U.S. edition © 2002 by Gareth Stevens, Inc.
Additional end matter © 2002 by Gareth Stevens, Inc.

Designer: Rob Shone
Editor: James Pickering
Picture Research: Carrie Haines

Gareth Stevens Editor: Jim Mezzanotte

Photo Credits:
Abbreviations: (t) top, (m) middle, (b) bottom, (l) left, (r) right

Milein Cosman/Lebrecht Collection: pages 5(tr), 24(tr), 25(bl).
Mike Evans/Lebrecht Collection: page 9(t).
David Farrell/Lebrecht Collection: page 8(tr).
B. Freeman/Lebrecht Collection: page 9(mr).
Hulton Getty: pages 21(tr), 26(mr), 28(tr, bl).
Lebrecht Collection: pages 7(mr), 9(br), 25(tr), 26(bl), 27(tm), 29(ml, br).
Andre LeCoz/Lebrecht Collection: pages 6-7(b), 27(b).
G. MacDomnic/Lebrecht Collection: page 8(b).
Popperfoto: cover (m), pages 4(b), 5(b), 10(bl).
Redferns: cover (br), pages 7(t) (Martin Langer); 4(t), 5(m), 10(m), 16(t), 16(b), 17(all), 19(bl, br),
  20(bl), 22(b), 23(ml) (Michael Ochs Archive); 3, 13(tr, br), 15(tl), 18(tr), 22(tr), 23(tr) (David
  Redfern); 10-11(b) (Chuck Boyd); 10(t) (Astrid Kirchherr); 12(bl) (S&G Press Agency); 12-13(m)
  (Glenn A. Baker); 13(tl), 14(ml) (Val Wilmer); 14(b) (Dick Barnata); 14(t) (Robert Johnson); 15(b)
  (Chuck Stewart); 18(b) (Gai Terrell); 19(mt) (Keith Morris); 21(ml) (Elliott Landy); 21(mb) (Herb
  Green); 23(br) (Andrew Putler); 25(br) (David Farrell); 20(tr) (WHO: RB6919); 11(tl).
Rex Features: pages 6(m), 11(br).
Alex Sobolewski: page 24(bl).
Greg Tomin/Lebrecht Collection: page 29(tl).

Printed in the United States of America

1 2 3 4 5 6 7 8 9 06 05 04 03 02

20TH CENTURY *music*

1960s

THE AGE OF ROCK

Malcolm Hayes

Gareth Stevens Publishing
A WORLD ALMANAC EDUCATION GROUP COMPANY

CONTENTS

In the 1960s, many popular musicians became more than just entertainers. Bob Dylan's songs and performances, which had a tough, cutting edge, were often protests against war and the conventions of society.

The hippie way of life in the 1960s blended escapism with rebellion. It involved "dropping out" of the social and financial obligations of traditional society and "turning on" to different values, including those of rock music.

FREEDOM AND REBELLION

The 1960s were a time of progress and protest. The United States and other developed, democratic countries experienced economic prosperity, and great strides were made in technology and other fields. Yet prosperity was accompanied by turmoil and change. In the United States, the stream of U.S. troops being sent to South Vietnam, which the United States was backing in its war against communist North Vietnam, sparked widespread protests, and racial tensions also exploded across the country. While communist governments in the Soviet Union and Eastern Europe continued to suppress the freedoms of their citizens, young people in the United States and many Western European countries rebelled against the social conventions of the time, adopting new ways of both thinking and living.

The music of the 1960s also broke with past traditions as it searched for new sounds. Popular music, in particular, was transformed by a new generation of rock musicians who came to symbolize the era's hopes and dreams.

During the 1960s, in his final years, Igor Stravinsky wrote some forward-looking masterpieces.

Led by Diana Ross (center), the Supremes *were the most successful female vocal group of the 1960s. Ross later went solo.*

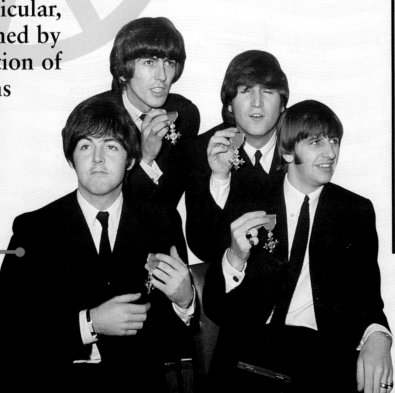

Hugely popular, the Beatles all received medals from the Queen of England in 1965.

CLASSICAL STEW

By the 1960s, the motto in classical music was "anything goes." A huge, confusing variety of traditional and modern styles and techniques was now available to composers. More than ever before, only the most powerfully gifted individuals could succeed.

THE MASTER AT WORK

France's Olivier Messiaen (1908–1992) matched the younger generation's adventurousness while remaining true to his two great inspirations, the Catholic faith and the world of nature. The awesome grandeur of *Et Exspecto Resurrectionem Mortuorum*, or *And I Await the Resurrection of the Dead*, (1964) was inspired by the biblical Book of Revelation. In 1969, Messiaen completed his vast, ten-movement oratorio *La Transfiguration de Notre-Seigneur Jésus-Christ*.

CHANCE AND CHOICE

Frenchman Pierre Boulez (b. 1925) became increasingly important as a conductor while continuing to compose. His main project was *Pli selon Pli*, or *Fold on Fold*, (1962, with later revisions), a hugely complicated orchestral work involving aleatory, or "chance," techniques. Jean Barraqué (1928–1973), also from France, explored a musical idiom that was more radical in tone but broader and more spacious in *Chant après Chant*, or *Song after Song*, (1966) and in his Clarinet Concerto (1968).

ROCK CONTACTS

Karlheinz Stockhausen (b. 1928), from Germany, created avant-garde works that were often close in spirit to rock music. *Kontakte*, or *Contacts*, (1960), for piano, percussion, and electronic tape, and *Stimmung*, or *Tuning and/or Mood*, (1968) are both 1960s classics. Stockhausen knew Paul McCartney, and his ideas may have influenced such later Beatles albums as *Sergeant Pepper's Lonely Hearts Club Band*.

The music of Messiaen had a large following among composers as well as listeners.

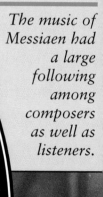

Stockhausen's works often involved suggestions for improvising rather than actual musical notes.

György Ligeti settled in Vienna, where his music explored new and often beautiful possibilities for the collective sound of instruments.

Pierre Boulez rehearses Stravinsky's The Rite of Spring *in 1963. In the 1960s, Boulez expressed his radical musical views both in his own compositions and in his high-profile work as an international conductor.*

OPERA AND OTHER DARING EXPERIMENTS

Die Soldaten, or *The Soldiers* (1960), an opera by Germany's Bernd Alois Zimmermann (1918–1970), is a bleak story about the corrupting effect of militarism on the human spirit. It involves complex staging and images projected on to multiple screens. Hungarian exile György Ligeti (*b*. 1923) created music that blended melody and harmony in rippling tapestries of sound, as in his orchestral *Atmosphères* (1961) and *Lontano*, or *Distant*, (1967) and the 1965 choral piece *Requiem*. Ligeti also explored a kind of sound theater in *Aventures* and *Nouvelles Aventures* (both 1966). Greek composer Iannis Xenakis (1922–2001) combined mathematical complexity with fiery power. His major works include the fiendishly difficult *Eonta*, or *Being*, (1964), for piano and brass, and *Nuits*, or *Nights*, (1968), for unaccompanied chorus.

BRITISH COMPOSERS

As an island nation off the coast of the European continent, Britain has typically been a part of Europe and yet separate from it. In the 1960s, British composers reflected this condition. While taking notice of developments on mainland Europe, they also followed their own unique paths.

BRITTEN AT HOME

While planning and directing the Aldeburgh Festival, located on the Suffolk coast where he lived, Benjamin Britten (1913–1976) composed as fluently as ever. Britten's operas include *A Midsummer Night's Dream* (1960) and a set of three Church Parables (1964–1968). *War Requiem* (1961) was an oratorio with a remarkable difference. Besides the Latin words of the Requiem Mass, Britten included poems by British poet Wilfred Owen, who served and died in World War I.

DIFFERENT DIRECTIONS

Michael Tippett (1905–1998) explored harder-edged territory than he previously had with *King Priam* (1961), an opera based on Homer's *Iliad*, an ancient Greek poem about the Trojan War. Malcolm Arnold (*b.* 1921), famous as a film composer, continued a fine cycle of symphonies with his Fourth and Fifth Symphonies (1960). Catalan exile Roberto Gerhard (1896–1970) wrote his brilliant Concerto for Orchestra (1965), as well as his chamber works *Libra* (1968) and *Leo* (1969).

A nun dressed in red screams into a megaphone in Peter Maxwell Davies's Revelation and Fall. It made extreme demands on its performers.

Britten conducts at the London Proms (Promenade Concerts). In the 1960s, Britten was firmly established as his country's leading classical composer. A superb pianist, he often played chamber music at the Aldeburgh Festival.

8

Michael Tippett's visionary, mystical The Midsummer Marriage (1955) had been little understood or appreciated until its production at London's Royal Opera House in 1969. The huge success of both the production and its recording helped make the British composer internationally famous.

FASTEN YOUR SEAT BELTS

Peter Maxwell Davies (*b.* 1934) took the atonal style of Arnold Schoenberg (1874–1951) to ferocious new heights with his *Revelation and Fall* (1966), which was based on the nightmare visions of Austrian poet Georg Trakl, and his orchestral *Worldes Blis*, or World's Bliss, (1969). Harrison Birtwistle (*b.* 1934) managed to both outrage and impress audiences with extremes of harshness and lyrical beauty in his *Tragoedia* (1965), for chamber orchestra, and his opera *Punch and Judy* (1968).

Harrison Birtwistle achieved the uncompromising, startlingly original sounds in such works as Tragoedia, Punch and Judy, and Verses for Ensembles (1969) by combining a hard-edged, avant-garde style with techniques adapted from medieval classical music.

WALTON IN ITALY

In the later years of his life, William Walton (1902–1983) lived on the Italian island of Ischia. The tone of his later music was subtler and more refined than that of his earlier works. Besides two masterly creations, his Second Symphony (1960) and Variations on a Theme by Hindemith (1963), Walton also completed a witty one-act opera, *The Bear* (1967).

The Aragonese Castle off the island of Ischia

THE BEATLES

In July 1957, Paul McCartney (*b.* 1942), a young and guitarist from Liverpool, England, met anothe aspiring musician, John Lennon (1940–1980). Wi three years they had become the nucleus of the Be one of the most successful pop groups of all time.

The Beatles lineup in 1960 included Pete Best (far left) and Stu Sutcliffe (far right).

George Mar from right), t highly i record poses with McCartney, Starr, an

EARLY DAYS

By 1960, Lennon and McCartney had been joined by lead guitarist George Harrison (1943–2001), bassist Stu Sutcliffe, and drummer Pete Best. The group spent a lot of time in Hamburg, Germany. When Sutcliffe left, McCartney soon switched to bass. Back in England, Ringo Starr (*b.* Richard Starkey, 1940) took over on drums in 1962.

Brian Epstein (far left), the Beatles' manager, appears with the group on The Ed Sullivan Show in 1964. The Beatles never really recovered from his death in 1967.

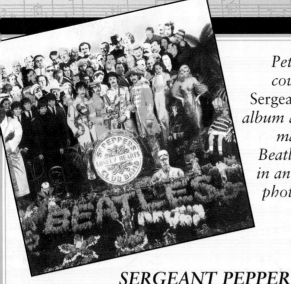

Peter Blake's cover for the Sergeant Pepper *album assembled many of the Beatles' heroes in an elaborate photo collage.*

SERGEANT PEPPER

By mid-1967, the Beatles had stopped touring. They were not able to hear themselves above the screaming of their audiences, and there had also been death threats. The Beatles were now able to focus all of their energy on recording new songs. The result was the groundbreaking album *Sergeant Pepper's Lonely Hearts Club Band.* "Lucy in the Sky with Diamonds," "A Day in the Life," and other songs set a new standard for popular music.

McCartney (left) *and Lennon were two very different songwriters. While they sometimes argued, the combination of their talents produced brilliant results.*

ULTIMATE TALENT, ULTIMATE FAME

In 1964, "Beatlemania" swept the United States, and the "Fab Four" had five singles at the top of the U.S. charts. Lennon and McCartney (and sometimes Harrison) were now writing almost all of the Beatles' songs, which marked a new trend in popular music. While Lennon often provided a sharp edge to the band's music, McCartney drew together rock and pop influences and created his own brand of gentle ballad. By 1966, the group's hits ranged from such early singles as "From Me to You" and "Can't Buy Me Love" to such albums as *Beatles for Sale* (1964), *Help!* (1965), *Rubber Soul* (1965), and the boldly adventurous *Revolver* (1966). The Beatles also starred in the films *A Hard Day's Night* (1964) and *Help!* (1965).

FINAL CHAPTER

After the Beatles reached new heights with *Sergeant Pepper's Lonely Hearts Club Band* (1967), tensions in the group began to mount. Despite their problems, the group managed to release *The Beatles* (1968, known as the "White Album"), *Abbey Road* (1969), and *Let It Be* (1970), before calling it quits in April 1970.

The "Fab Four" pose for one of their last pictures together at the house of John Lennon (far left) *in 1969.*

ENGLAND ROCKS AMERICA

The Beatles' massive success in North America was a landmark for popular music. Before the Beatles, the story of twentieth-century popular music had been about the impact of American music — blues, jazz, rock 'n' roll — on Europe. Now the tide of influence was flowing the other way.

A SPECIAL CITY

Much of 1960s rock had its roots in Liverpool. Located on the Mersey River, Liverpool is different from other British cities — more freewheeling and cosmopolitan, with a large Irish community with many links to the United States. Before the Beatles came along, such "Merseyside" groups as Gerry and the Pacemakers were making the transition from 1950s rock 'n' roll to 1960s pop. Liverpool native Cilla Black also found fame as a singer before embarking on a successful career in television.

Gerry and the Pacemakers perform at Liverpool's Cavern Club, where the Beatles also played. The group was the first in Britain to get three No. 1 hits on the British charts with their first three singles.

THE STONES ARRIVE

After forming in London in 1962, the Rolling Stones eventually dominated 1960s rock 'n' roll almost as completely as the Beatles. Fusing rock and blues in their own provocative way, the Stones scored a huge hit in Britain and North America with "(I Can't Get No) Satisfaction" (1965). Keith Richards's guitar-playing, Mick Jagger's aggressive vocals, and Charlie Watts's tight drumming are still at the heart of the group's superstardom.

Rolling Stones (from left) Charlie Watts, Bill Wyman, Brian Jones, Keith Richards, and Mick Jagger pose for an early photograph.

BRITISH POP TAKES OFF

The success of the Beatles paved the way for many other British performers who, as part of the "British Invasion," also found appreciative U.S. audiences. The Dave Clark Five, who were often compared to the Beatles, scored many hits, as did Manfred Mann (whose band included Jack Bruce, the future bassist for the influential rock trio Cream), the Hollies, and Herman's Hermits.

Manfred Mann (far left) *led his group from his keyboard, while* Paul Jones (center) *supplied the vocals.*

13

AMONG THE BEST

The Animals were formed in the English city of Newcastle in 1964 with a lineup that centered on the powerful vocals of Eric Burdon and the keyboard work of Alan Price. That year, the band's version of the traditional ballad "House of the Rising Sun" topped both the British and U.S. charts. This success was followed by more hit singles, worldwide tours, and such popular albums as *The Animals* (1964), *Animal Tracks* (1965), and *Animalism* (1966).

Animals (from left) *Hilton Valentine, Alan Price, Eric Burdon, John Steel, and Chas Chandler appear on the television show* Ready, Steady, Go!

BLUES REBORN

In the 1960s, many rock musicians were influenced by the blues, an American art form that first emerged among blacks in the rural South and then traveled up to such northern cities as Chicago. Rock musicians incorporated traditional blues styles but also took the blues in new directions.

MUSICAL CHAIRS

As the 1960s progressed, blues bands in Britain saw many different personnel changes. The Yardbirds formed in London in 1961, and over the years their lineup included guitarists Eric Clapton (who later formed Cream), Jeff Beck, and Jimmy Page (who later formed Led Zeppelin). On *Bluesbreakers with Eric Clapton* (1966), keyboard ace John Mayall's Bluesbreakers included bassist John McVie. Along with Peter Green and Mick Fleetwood, both of whom also played with Mayall at various times, McVie formed the group Fleetwood Mac.

The recordings of blues great Robert Johnson (1911–1938) inspired many young musicians in the 1960s.

After leaving the Yardbirds, Eric Clapton (far right) played with John Mayall's Bluesbreakers. He then formed Cream.

The British rock group Led Zeppelin, (from left) John Paul Jones, Jimmy Page, Robert Plant, and John Bonham, recorded its first album in just two weeks.

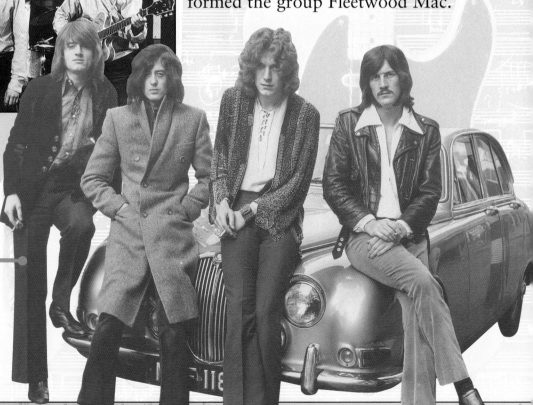

14

SUPREME GUITARIST

Seattle native Jimi Hendrix (1942–1970) toured with the Isley Brothers and rock 'n' roll star Little Richard. He was then spotted by Chas Chandler, a former bassist for the Animals who had turned to producing. Chandler brought Hendrix to England, where the Jimi Hendrix Experience was formed with bassist Noel Redding and drummer Mitch Mitchell. Hendrix's dazzling guitar-playing had already made him a legend by the time of his tragic early death.

Over thirty years after his death, many people still consider Jimi Hendrix the finest electric guitarist ever.

WE ARE THE CREAM

Cream came together in 1966 and disbanded just two years later. By then a legend had been created by the combination of Eric Clapton's virtuoso guitar work, Ginger Baker's powerful drumming, and the inventive bass playing of Jack Bruce, who also sang and played the harmonica. Bruce, who was classically trained, once said that his bass lines were influenced by those of Johann Sebastian Bach (1685–1750). Cream's album *Disraeli Gears* (1967) was a huge success, as was the double album *Wheels of Fire* (1968), which included a live set from the Fillmore West in San Francisco.

THE ZEPPELIN IS AIRBORNE

In 1968, Jimmy Page formed the New Yardbirds with bassist and keyboardist John Paul Jones. With vocalist Robert Plant and drummer John Bonham on board, they renamed themselves Led Zeppelin. With the release of its first album, *Led Zeppelin* (1969), the group launched a blues-based style of hard rock that would dominate the 1970s.

In Cream, Jack Bruce (left), Ginger Baker (center), and Eric Clapton performed as a trio of equals. Their playing was at its most exciting when each member was fighting the others for the lead.

AMERICAN SOUL

Like blues and jazz, soul music is as much about a feeling and a state of mind as about a particular style. The music first surfaced in the United States in the 1950s as a type of jazz that reflected the influence of gospel music — which itself has roots in hymns and spirituals.

STAX AND MOTOWN

By the 1960s, soul had become a music of many different influences, with elements of gospel rubbing shoulders with rhythm-and-blues. Soul also became the unofficial musical voice of the civil rights movement in the United States. Its success was fueled by the "house styles" of two dominant record labels. In Detroit, producer Berry Gordy, Jr., ran Motown Records, which had hits with Marvin Gaye, the Supremes, and others. Stax Records, in Memphis, made its mark with such singers as Otis Redding (1941–1967).

Led by Diana Ross (center), the Supremes had a string of hits in the 1960s, including "Baby Love" (1964) and "You Keep Me Hangin' On" (1966).

More than just a singer, Otis Redding was a producer, talent scout, and songwriter for Stax Records before he was killed in a plane crash. His albums include Otis Blue *and* The Blue Album *(both 1966).*

THE GODFATHER AND THE QUEEN

With a gritty, powerful voice that was propelled by the raw rhythmic energy of his band, James Brown (*b.* 1933) became the "Godfather of Soul." He also helped create funk, an offshoot of soul that was even more focused on infectious rhythms. Aretha Franklin grew up singing gospel music and never lost her gospel roots. Her masterful combination of passion and tremendous vocal skill made her the undisputed "Queen of Soul."

James Brown opened up new territory with his explosive, rhythm-based vocal style, as in "Let Yourself Go" and "Cold Sweat" in 1967 and "Say it Loud — I'm Black and I'm Proud" in 1968.

MORE SOUL STARS

A gifted, versatile singer and songwriter, Marvin Gaye (1939–1984) was able to bring jazz elements into a broad musical spectrum that ranged from gospel to funk. Diana Ross (*b.* 1944) and her all-female group, the Supremes, also built a huge following. The Isley Brothers created an enthusiastic mix of soul and rhythm-and-blues. Their 1962 single "Twist and Shout" became a big hit for the Beatles the following year.

STEVIE WONDER

Blind from birth, Steveland Morris Judkins (*b.* 1950) was a fluent pianist, harmonica-player, and drummer by the age of ten. Signed by Motown in 1962 and billed as "Little Stevie Wonder," he had a number one hit that year with "Fingertips (Part 2)" and soon became a star as both a singer and a songwriter.

Stevie Wonder's first album was The 12 Year Old Genius (1962).

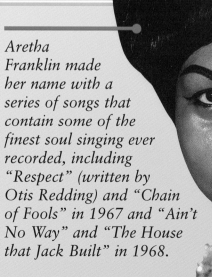

Aretha Franklin made her name with a series of songs that contain some of the finest soul singing ever recorded, including "Respect" (written by Otis Redding) and "Chain of Fools" in 1967 and "Ain't No Way" and "The House that Jack Built" in 1968.

SINGERS AND SONGWRITERS

The age of freedom and resistance produced musicians who could give voice to the dreams and desires of a new generation. These singers and songwriters were the wandering minstrels of their time.

AMERICAN TROUBADOUR

Bob Dylan (*b*. Robert Zimmerman, 1941) quickly made his name as the leading folksinger of his generation. He wrote his own songs, which often had complex and bitter lyrics with a sharp political slant, and he used electric as well as acoustic guitars. *Highway 61 Revisited* (1965) is a classic album of its period. After a motorcycle accident in 1966, Dylan's tone changed. *John Wesley Harding* (1968) shows the gentler influence of country music, with many references to the Bible.

Simon (left) and Garfunkel first met at school.

SIMON AND GARFUNKEL

The influence of 1950s stars the Everly Brothers can be heard in the close-harmony duets of singer, songwriter, and guitarist Paul Simon (*b*. 1941) and vocalist Art Garfunkel (*b*. 1941). The New York duo's folk-rock success began with "The Sounds of Silence" (1966). Their album *Parsley, Sage, Rosemary and Thyme* (1966) became the basis for Simon's score for the film *The Graduate* (1968). *Bookends* (1968) was their 1960s masterpiece.

Bob Dylan and Joan Baez sing together at the 1963 Newport Folk Festival.

18

VOICES OF AMERICA

With her anti-establishment political views, Joan Baez (b. 1941) came to symbolize the U.S. civil rights movement for many people. Janis Joplin (1943–1970) was an explosive, gritty blues singer. Joplin's spectacular vocal performances brought her huge success, and her records spent months at the top of the charts even after her early death.

Janis Joplin's passionate blues can be heard on Cheap Thrills *(1968) and* Pearl *(released in 1971, after her death).*

CALIFORNIA DREAMING

Formed in 1961 in Los Angeles, the Beach Boys expressed the early 1960s California dream of sun, surfing, and cruising around in cars. Their first hit was "Surfin' Safari" (1962). Brian Wilson, one of three brothers in the group, emerged as a talented songwriter. Another L.A. band, the Byrds, created a new sound with their shimmering version of Dylan's "Mr. Tambourine Man" in 1965. The original Byrds lineup included David Crosby, who in 1968 joined fellow singer-songwriters Stephen Stills and Graham Nash.

the mid-1960s, the Beach Boys had become more experimental. et Sounds (1966) influenced the eatles' Sergeant Pepper's Lonely Hearts Club Band.

The Byrds' style, based on folk, rock, and country, influenced the Beatles on such albums as Rubber Soul *and* Revolver.

ROCK GETS COSMIC

As technology — particularly recording technology — raced ahead, rock musicians began to push the limits of the musical imagination. One result of this experimentation was a blending of rock with the forms and resources of classical music.

ROCK MEETS CLASSICAL

British group the Moody Blues linked rock pieces with interludes for symphony orchestra on their *Days of Future Passed* (1968). The Who were already notorious as one of England's wildest rock bands when guitarist and songwriter Pete Townshend created his rock opera, *Tommy*, in 1969. American Frank Zappa brought together such diverse influences as rhythm-and-blues and the classical modernism of Stravinsky. The result was such startling albums as *Lumpy Gravy* (1968) and *Uncle Meat* (1969).

FLEETWOOD MAC IS LAUNCHED

The British group Fleetwood Mac was formed in 1969 by former Bluesbreakers Mick Fleetwood (drums), Peter Green (guitar and vocals), and John McVie (bass). They scored their first major hit single with "Albatross." London's Pink Floyd introduced a futuristic world of sound to listeners with their album *Piper at the Gates of Dawn* (1967). After this album, Pink Floyd's brilliant but troubled songwriter, Syd Barrett, left the group.

Pink Floyd, (clockwise from top left) Roger Waters, Syd Barrett, Rick Wright, and Nick Mason, was an early user of light shows in its stage act.

Pete Townshend's rock opera, Tommy, explored the world from the viewpoint of a "deaf, dumb, and blind boy." The title role was sung by Roger Daltrey (left), The Who's lead singer. In the 1970s, Tommy was turned into both a film starring Daltrey and a successful stage musical.

ROCK AND CLASSICAL COME TOGETHER

The British rock group Deep Purple surprised and impressed many people with an ambitious blend of rock and classical in their Concerto for Group and Orchestra (1969). The concerto was written by Deep Purple's classically trained keyboard player, Jon Lord. Malcolm Arnold scored the orchestral accompaniment and conducted the work at London's 1969 Promenade Concerts.

Arnold (conducting) rehearses the concerto by Lord (on keyboards).

EXOTIC WORLDS

Folk, blues, and wild experimentation came together in the music of San Franciso's Jefferson Airplane. Female lead singers in 1960s rock bands were rare, but the vocals and songwriting of the group's Grace Slick were highlighted on the albums *Surrealistic Pillow* (1967) and *Crown of Creation* (1968).

The Grateful Dead, another San Francisco band, released *Anthem of the Sun* (1968) and *Aoxomoxo* (1969). Both featured the daring work of keyboard player Tom Constanten, who studied with Boulez and other avant-garde artists.

21

The Doors formed in Los Angeles in 1965. Their musical voyages, at times both dark and dreamlike, were led by singer and songwriter Jim Morrison, who died in 1971.

The Haight-Ashbury district of San Francisco was where the hippie and "flower power" movements began. Pictured here in their native city are the Grateful Dead, one of rock's longest-lived groups. Surviving members of the band still play today.

JAZZ IN THE SIXTIES

Jazz in the 1960s mirrored the increasingly exotic experiments of the rock world. Leading jazz players explored new musical frontiers, building on the complex, improvised freedoms of bebop and the radical sounds of the classical avant-garde.

FREE-FORM JAZZ

Alto and tenor saxophonist Ornette Coleman (b. 1930) opened up a new world of jazz performance, playing in a quartet without a piano or guitar. In *This is Our Music* and *Free Jazz* (both 1960), saxes, trumpet, bass, and drums are all melodic soloists at the same time, without a supporting harmonic accompaniment.

AN ADVENTUROUS TALENT

John Coltrane (1926–1967) became a star after playing tenor saxophone in groups led by jazz greats Dizzy Gillespie (1917–1993) and Miles Davis (1926–1991). He now took "hard bop" jazz into the advanced harmonic world of the avant-garde, with elaborate improvisations that became known as "sheets of sound" and were partly inspired by his interest in Eastern and African music. Coltrane's religious beliefs were vividly expressed in his legendary album *A Love Supreme* (1965).

John Coltrane anticipated the fusion jazz of the 1970s by welcoming the influence of musicians from other cultures.

RAHSAAN ROLAND KIRK

Blind almost from birth, Rahsaan Roland Kirk (1936–1977) mastered the feat of playing three saxophones — a tenor and two unusual kinds of saxophone known as a stritchophone and a manzello — all at once. The idea had come to him in a dream. Kirk worked out a way to finger all three together, playing a three-part harmony whose sound was unique.

The name "Rahsaan" came to Roland Kirk in a dream.

Miles Davis's prolific output of recordings in the 1960s included the classic albums ESP *(1965) and* Sorceror *(1967). The Complete Concert (1964) was recorded live at New York City's Philharmonic Hall.*

Art Blakey formed his drumming style in the swing era, but he took it into the new age of bebop and progressive jazz with brilliant results. His finest albums include Free For All *(1965) and* Kyoto *(1968).*

THE MASTERS AND THE RISING STARS

In the late 1960s, Miles Davis began to explore new territories of jazz-rock fusion. He played trumpet and flugelhorn with keyboardists such as Chick Corea (*b.* 1941), Herbie Hancock (*b.* 1940), and Joe Zawinul (*b.* 1932), as well as with guitarist John McLaughlin (*b.* 1942), on albums such as *In a Silent Way* (1969). Many present and future stars of the jazz world, including Chick Corea, played hard bop jazz with a group called the Jazz Messengers, which was led by virtuoso drummer Art Blakey (1919–1990).

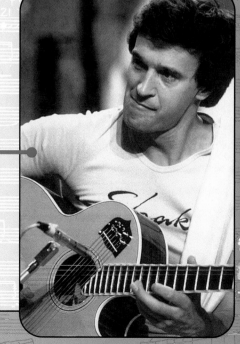

British guitarist John McLaughlin played with such rock musicians as guitarist Eric Clapton and drummer Ginger Baker. He then began working in New York City, contributing to Miles Davis's In a Silent Way.

S TRAVINSKY TO CAGE

American classical composers in the 1960s were led by a gifted older generation whose styles varied as much as American life itself. Russian native Igor Stravinsky (1882–1971), who had become a U.S. citizen, was their remarkable figurehead.

CARTER'S ADVANCED ENERGY

Elliott Carter (*b.* 1908) had developed a style of composing as complex as that of the European avant-garde, but the tone of his music was different. Carter's Double Concerto for Harpsichord, Piano and Two Chamber Orchestras (1961), Piano Concerto (1965), and Concerto for Orchestra (1969) were all highly dramatic works in a quite traditional sense. Beethoven would have recognized the underlying ideas, if not the style.

STILL THE GREATEST

In his final years, Stravinsky composed some brilliant music, adapting the serial technique pioneered by Arnold Schoenberg to his own musical style. *A Sermon, a Narrative and a Prayer* (1961) and *Requiem Canticles* (1966) are among the finest works he ever wrote.

Stravinsky conducts, as drawn by Milein Cosman.

Elliott Carter (right) *developed the intricate composing technique of "metric modulation," where a work's momentum is controlled by different layers of music that are performed simultaneously. Some layers start slowly and accelerate while other, quicker layers slow down.*

CAGE'S QUIET REBELLION

For decades, composer John Cage (1912–1992) had been exploring the outer reaches of what Western classical music seemed able to include. Cage found a connection between Eastern ways of thinking, such as Zen Buddhism, and the aleatory ("chance") devices of his own music. Examples of Cage's "happenings," which are actually precisely organized, include *Cartridge Music* (1960), based on the random amplified scratchings of an LP stylus, and *HPSCHD* (1969), for harpsichord sounds on computer-manipulated tape.

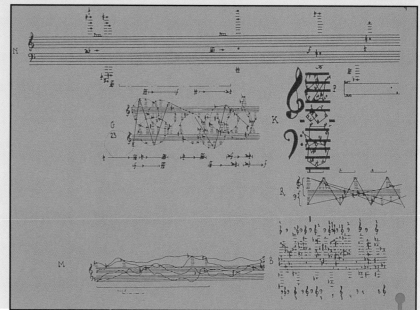

John Cage's Piano Concerto gives the player wide latitude to improvise notes and the order of events within particular musical guidelines.

AMERICAN MASTERS

At the height of his busy career as a conductor, Leonard Bernstein (1918–1990) still found time to compose his Third Symphony (*Kaddish*, 1963) and *Chichester Psalms* (1965). The film version of his musical *West Side Story* was released in 1961. Aaron Copland (1900–1990) wrote a ballet, *Dance Panels* (1963). He also wrote two orchestral works, *Connotation* (1962) and *Inscape* (1967).

Besides his composing, Bernstein also had a spectacular career conducting the New York Philharmonic Orchestra. He was their first (and so far only) American-born music director.

Aaron Copland (as drawn by Milein Cosman) wrote "advanced" works besides more listener-friendly pieces.

ITALIAN RADICALS

Beneath its stylish and increasingly prosperous surface, Italy in the 1960s was a nation of growing political conflict, as right-wing parties tied to the Catholic Church clashed with left-wing communists. The music of its composers often reflected this struggle.

WAYS OF EXPRESSION

Musical radicalism can come out in very different ways. The approach of Luciano Berio (*b.* 1925) was to find the essence of how music expresses itself in different techniques and styles. Like many of Berio's vocal works, *Epifanie* (1961), a song-cycle with orchestra, was written for his wife, the American soprano Cathy Berberian (1925–1983). Berio's *Sinfonia* (1969) was composed for the popular Swingle Singers and an orchestra. It quotes music by Gustav Mahler (1860–1911), Schoenberg, and other composers within the context of Berio's own music.

REBEL WITH A CAUSE

For Luigi Nono (1924–1990), radical politics related to his own individual development of Schoenberg's serial method. At the premiere of his one-act opera *Intolleranza 1960*, or *Intolerance 1960*, in Venice, there were street demonstrations between left- and right-wing groups. *Per Bastiana Tai-Yang Cheng*, or *For Bastiana* [Nono's daughter] *the East Is Red*, (1967), for orchestra and electronic tape, was Nono's salute to communist China.

For Luigi Nono, music and message were one.

Cathy Berberian, who was married to Luciano Berio from 1950 to 1966, was a trained dancer and mime as well as a singer. She excelled in avant-garde music. Berio composed several works for her, including Circles *(1960), for soprano, harp, and percussion, and* Sequenza III *(1966), for solo voice.*

26

AN ANCIENT STORY RETOLD

Luigi Dallapiccola (1904–1975) spent most of the 1960s working on his crowning masterpiece, the large-scale opera *Ulisse*, or *Ulysses*, (1968). The opera tells the story of the Greek hero Odysseus (Ulysses), from the *Odyssey* by the ancient Greek poet Homer. In the opera's epilogue, Dallapiccola adds a Christian message: Ulysses, the perpetual wanderer, first becomes aware of God. The music's tone is mostly quiet, but it still has great power.

As Dallapiccola had intended, Ulisse summed up his musical life. His other works from the 1960s include Parole di San Paolo, *or Words of St. Paul, (1964), for soprano and chamber group.*

AN AVANT-GARDIST WITH CHARM

Maderna's own music remains overshadowed by his reputation as a conductor. Besides new works, Maderna's repertory included many other pieces, notably Mahler's symphonies.

Bruno Maderna (1920–1973) was famous as a conductor, often of avant-garde works by his contemporaries, but he was also a fine composer. Like Berio, Nono, and Dallapiccola, he was able to blend advanced techniques with attractive sounds. Two of Maderna's three oboe concertos were composed in 1962 and 1967. *Quadrivium* (1969), for percussion quartet and orchestra, is more radical music.

REPRESSION AND RESISTANCE

Life in the Soviet Union and Eastern Europe was very different from that in Western democracies. Communist governments controlled and often sharply restricted freedoms, including cultural freedoms. In Poland, however, the communist authorities slightly loosened their grip on music.

Polish hippies try hitching a ride outside the capital of Poland, Warsaw. The notice says "Driver, help the child."

Soviet leader Nikita Krushchev, who succeeded Joseph Stalin, relaxed Soviet control in Eastern Europe, but not by much.

NEW POSSIBILITIES

Most countries in Eastern Europe insisted that music should serve the cause of "Socialist realism," which meant composing conventional works that did not involve experimentation. But Polish authorities took a different view. They responded to the rise of the Western avant-garde by giving their own composers a chance to compete with it. In Poland, radical modernism, far from being repressed, was suddenly a requirement.

NO COMPROMISE

The earlier years of Soviet persecution permanently marked Russian composer Dmitri Shostakovich (1906–1975). His Thirteenth Symphony (1962) was a setting of texts by the poet Yevgeny Yevtushenko criticizing aspects of Soviet Russia, especially its anti-Semitism. The Soviet authorities angrily postponed its first performance. The more private tone of Shostakovich's string quartets, nos. 8 to 12 (1960–1968), is dark and haunted.

Shostakovich stayed true to himself.

BARTÓK TO FREE RHYTHMS

When the official line changed in Poland, Witold Lutoslawski (1913–1994), whose early style related to that of Hungary's Béla Bartók (1881–1945), responded with *Venetian Games* (1961) for orchestra. The work contrasted sections constructed in aleatoric style, where the rhythms of the individual instruments are free, with sections that had strict rhythms. In his String Quartet (1964) and *Livre pour Orchestre*, or *Book for Orchestra*, (1968), Lutoslawski took this idea further.

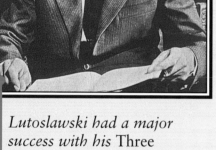

Lutoslawski had a major success with his Three Poems of Henri Michaux *(1963), for chorus, wind instruments, and percussion.*

Penderecki dedicated his choral Dies Irae *(1967) to the victims of the World War II concentration camp Auschwitz, where the work was first performed.*

A CHRISTIAN MODERNIST

Polish composer Krzysztof Penderecki (*b.* 1933) had a bold style that explored extremes of high and low registers, in dense slabs and clusters of choral and orchestral sound. Penderecki's *Threnody for the Victims of Hiroshima* (1960) for fifty-two solo strings was performed by orchestras all over the world. His large-scale, choral *St. Luke Passion* (1965) contrasted his interest in avant-garde sounds with a more traditional, chant-based style to tell the story of Christ's crucifixion and death.

· TIME LINE ·

	WORLD EVENTS	MUSICAL EVENTS	THE ARTS	FAMOUS MUSICIANS	MUSICAL WORKS
1960	• *John F. Kennedy elected U.S. president* • *U.S. spy plane downed over Russia*	• *The twist becomes a dance craze that sweeps the world*	• *Hitchcock:* Psycho • *Kubrick:* Spartacus • *Fellini:* La Dolce Vita	• *Death of Leonard Warren, American baritone singer*	• *Walton: Second Symphony* • *Lerner and Loewe:* Camelot
1961	• *Berlin Wall built* • *Yuri Gagarin is the first man in space* • *Bay of Pigs invasion of Cuba*	• *"Biggest Show of Stars" U.S. tour with Fats Domino, Chubby Checker, and the Drifters*	• *Dancer Rudolf Nureyev defects from the Soviet Union* • *Film version of* West Side Story *released*	• *Jazz trumpeter Wynton Marsalis is born*	• *Stravinsky:* A Sermon, a Narrative, and a Prayer • *Britten:* War Requiem
1962	• *Cuban missile crisis* • *Algeria gains independence from France*	• *The Beatles offered a recording contract* • *Premiere of Tippett's opera* King Priam	• *Anthony Burgess:* A Clockwork Orange • *David Lean:* Lawrence of Arabia	• *Country and western singer Garth Brooks is born*	• *Shostakovich: Thirteenth Symphony* • *The Beach Boys:* "Surfin' Safari"
1963	• *President Kennedy assassinated* • *Martin Luther King, Jr., fights for civil rights*	• *Joan Baez and Bob Dylan appear at Newport Folk Festival*	• *Neil Simon:* Barefoot in the Park • *Sean Connery stars in* From Russia with Love	• *Deaths of Paul Hindemith, Francis Poulenc, and Edith Piaf, French popular singer*	• *Messiaen:* Couleurs de la Cité Céleste • *The Beatles:* Please Please Me
1964	• *Palestinian Liberation Organization formed* • *UN sanctions against South Africa*	• *Richmond Jazz and Blues Festival in Britain stars the Rolling Stones*	• *Arthur Miller:* After the Fall • *Peter Sellers stars in* Dr. Strangelove	• *The Byrds are formed in Los Angeles* • *Topol stars in* Fiddler on the Roof	• *Stockhausen:* Momente • *My Fair Lady soundtrack*
1965	• *First U.S. combat troops land in Vietnam* • *India and Pakistan at war over Kashmir*	• *The Rolling Stones' "(I Can't Get No) Satisfaction" sweeps Britain and the United States*	• *Michael Caine stars in* The Ipcress File • *Death of T. S. Eliot, U.S.-born poet* • *Godard:* Alphaville	• *Death of jazz singer and pianist Nat "King" Cole*	• *The Who:* "My Generation" • *John Coltrane:* A Love Supreme
1966	• *Soviet Union lands unpiloted spacecraft on the Moon* • *China: cultural revolution begins*	• *The Beach Boys' album* Pet Sounds *features early electronic instruments*	• *Burton and Taylor star in* Who's Afraid of Virginia Woolf? • *Start of U.S. TV show* The Monkees	• *Italian mezzo-soprano Cecilia Bartoli is born* • *The Beatles stop touring*	• *Stravinsky:* Requiem Canticles • *Bob Dylan:* Blonde on Blonde
1967	• *Six-Day War between Israel and Arab nations*	• *BBC Radio One is launched* • *Monterey pop festival is held in California*	• *Dustin Hoffman stars in* The Graduate *by Mike Nichols*	• *Genesis is formed* • *Death of saxophonist John Coltrane*	• *Copland:* Inscape • *The Beatles:* Sergeant Pepper's Lonely Hearts Club Band
1968	• *Vietnam: Tet Offensive* • *Paris: student riots* • *Martin Luther King, Jr., is shot*	• *First albums from Deep Purple, Fleetwood Mac, and Jethro Tull*	• *Stanley Kubrick:* 2001: A Space Odyssey • *Broadway premiere of the musical* Hair	• *Syd Barrett quits Pink Floyd* • *Cream splits up*	• *Stockhausen:* Stimmung • *The Rolling Stones:* Beggars Banquet
1969	• *Neil Armstrong is the first man on the Moon* • *Concorde has its first flight*	• *450,000 people gather at Woodstock rock festival in upstate New York*	• *Peter Fonda and Dennis Hopper star in* Easy Rider	• *Death of The Rolling Stones' Brian Jones* • *Death of saxophonist Coleman Hawkins*	• *Shostakovich: Fourteenth Symphony* • *Frank Sinatra:* My Way

GLOSSARY

aleatory: referring to music whose order of notes, sections, or even whole movements is left to the performers to decide, sometimes during the performance itself.

avant-garde: relating to innovative works that challenge the boundaries of conventional arts.

bebop: a style of jazz involving a complex mix of melody, harmony, and rhythm.

chamber music: music for a small group of musicians, made to be performed in a room or small concert hall.

concerto: a work with three distinct movements that is written for a solo instrument and an orchestra.

flugelhorn: a brass instrument with the sound of a bugle but with the keys of a trumpet or cornet.

hard bop: a faster, more aggressive version of bebop.

harpsichord: a keyboard instrument whose strings are plucked, making a twanging sound.

oratorio: a work for solo voices, chorus, and orchestra, usually with a religious theme.

quartet: a work for four instruments; also, a group of four musicians.

serial: referring to a method of creating music that involves a different way of ordering notes.

soprano: the highest female singing voice; also, a type of saxophone with a particular tone.

symphony: a long piece of music, usually divided into several sections, written for a large orchestra.

tenor: the highest male singing voice; also, a type of saxophone with a particular tone.

troubadour: a traveling singer-songwriter in medieval Italy and France.

MORE BOOKS TO READ

Aretha Franklin. Black Americans of Achievement (series). Jim McAvoy (Chelsea House)

The Beatles. Trailblazers of the Modern World (series). Michael Burgan (World Almanac Library)

Folk and Blues: The Encyclopedia. Irwin Stambler and Lyndon Stambler (St. Martin's Press)

The History of Motown. African American Achievers (series). Virginia Aronson (Chelsea House)

Jazz: An American Saga. James Lincoln Collier (Henry Holt & Company)

Jimi Hendrix. They Died Too Young (series). Tom Stockdale (Chelsea House)

John Coltrane: Jazz Revolutionary. Masters of Music (series). Rachel Stiffler Barron (Morgan Reynolds)

John Lennon and Paul McCartney: Their Magic and Their Music. Partners II (series). Bruce Glassman (Blackbirch Marketing)

Leonard Bernstein: A Passion for Music. Johanna Hurwitz (Jewish Publication Society)

The Rolling Stones. People in the News (series). Stuart A. Kallen (Lucent Books)

WEB SITES

20th Century Music: John Cage.
www.emory.edu/MUSIC/ARNOLD/cage.html

Michael Tippett.
www.michael-tippett.com

Olivier Messiaen.
www.hnh.com/composer/messiaen.htm

Ornette Coleman.
www.eyeneer.com/Jazz/Ornette/index.html

Due to the dynamic nature of the Internet, some web sites stay current longer than others. To find additional web sites, use a reliable search engine with one or more of the following keywords: *Benjamin Britten, James Brown, Luigi Dallapiccola, Bob Dylan, Miles Davis, Krzysztof Penderecki, Dmitri Shostakovich,* and *Karlheinz Stockhausen.*

INDEX